100 Pets

Written by Sharon Fear

Illustrated by Mits Katayama

Ms. Honey's class was going to celebrate 100 days of school.

"On day 100,"
said Ms. Honey,
"I would like for you to bring
100 things to school.
You may decide what to bring."

The children talked it over.
After a while, they agreed upon
what they wanted to bring to school.

4

They told Ms. Honey their idea.

"One hundred pets?"
asked the teacher.

"Yes, Ms. Honey!"
said the children.

5

Ms. Honey tried to picture
100 pets in the classroom.

"Children," she said,
"I had in mind
something small, quiet, and clean."

7

"Will these pets be small and quiet?" asked Ms. Honey.

"Yes, Ms. Honey!" said the children.

"Will they be clean?" asked Ms. Honey.

"Yes, Ms. Honey!" said the children.

"Do you really have
100 pets?" asked the teacher.

"Yes, Ms. Honey!" said the class.
"We really do!"

Ms. Honey said in a sweet voice,
"Well...then...all right."

On day 100, the children brought in...
pictures of their 100 pets!

"What a clever idea!" said Ms. Honey.
"Let's put them up for everyone to see.
And then we'll count them to see
if there really are 100."

Leo had a picture of his two dogs.
Carla had a picture of her cat
and six kittens.
Cathy had a cockatiel.
Jan had a box turtle.
Jerry lived on a farm.
He had a pony, a goat, a puppy,
a little rooster, and six ducks.

"Oh my," said Ms. Honey.
"That's 21 pets!"

Marshall had two hamsters.
Tran had a parrot.
June had a ferret.

Larry had six rabbits, ten fish,
and three snails
that lived in a fishbowl.

"Oh my!" said Ms. Honey,
as she continued to count.
"That's 44 pets!"

Bob and Ann each had a frog.
Pat had a pair of parakeets,
and Gail had a guinea pig.
Abby had a lizard
that could change its color.

"Oh my!" said Ms. Honey.
"That's 50 pets!
But how can you ever
come up with 50 more?"

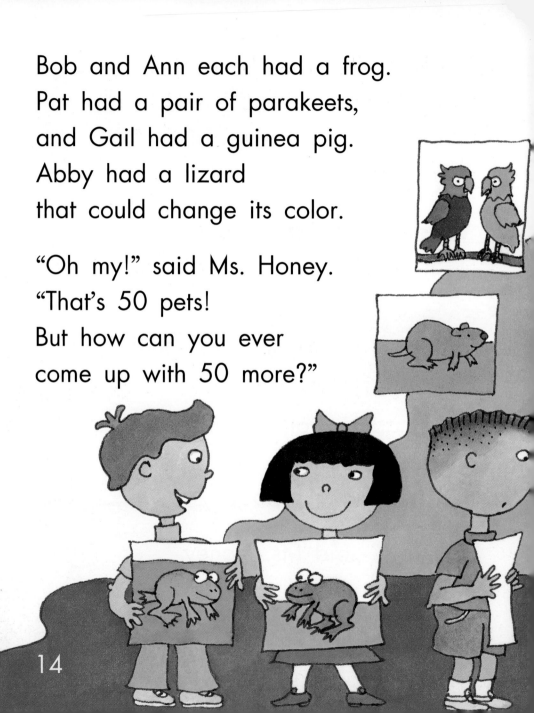

Just then the twins brought in
their ant farm with 50 ants in it.
"We brought in the real farm,"
said Norton.

"Because we didn't want
to draw 50 ants," said Horton.

"Oh my!" said Ms. Honey.
"You did it, children!
You brought in 100 pets!"

And they are all very small,
very quiet, and very clean.

16